ANNE MORRIGAN

BRUTAL WANDERER

ISBN 978-1-7387450-0-5 (paperback)

ISBN 978-1-7387450-1-2 (ebook)

Cover photo by Arianna Jadé

Text is set in Noto Serif Display and Red Hat Display

for andrew

forgive me, beautiful

I never thought to thank you

for all that living

contents

fingerprints only

on winter's first ice

linger a little longer

quick witted river

supple branches bend

dusting off soft snow

dark confidences

the fires, though long since ashen

keep my secrets still

the jay can't come in,

I can't go out—

two winters

my pieces grind together

like the plates of the earth

I lose momentum

I doubt myself

I don't

write

hair dryer

her damp edges

curled

snow falls gently on the trash in the yard

"Set a reminder for March first,"

your homeward footprints

not as marvellous

as fresh snow

snowed in with the Buddha

the loudest silent night

winter's welcome worn out

I shovel in silence

steam turns to ice

in tendrils down these thighs

arthritic fingers of frost

reaching into empty night

waking without the sun

unrest

winter solstice

Lawren Harris paints an arctic landscape

on our rural backyard

separate—

so similar to other nights

but with the different me

silent as you go

leaving fingerprints only

traces of the unsaid

the child with the wreath

is as tall as her mother's headstone

from above

to on

to in

with one misstep

the frozen ground

resisting sleep

of the long night moon

unsure if the sun will rise

so long, loneliness

setting my bed on fire

just to feel the heat

northerly wind

relaxed, then

your name

darkness between days

sleepless, I think

black thoughts

your skin isn't seamless—

you crawled in through a gash

to gain a second life

inhabiting the shadow

of the one who dissolved

at the heeding of a knife

whole loneliness full

a life of meaningless days

spent all wandering

compressed within

the weighted blanket silence

cut threads

deep cut and run

chasing down the knave

of an abrupt change of heart

hostile architecture

washing our hands of human debris

one desperation

unfurls into another

with such agony

disappointing world

where little hands hold sorrow

instead of stardust

ice shards lace the wind

frost bleeds from dirt

to brick, to bone

the grip of winter

tightens on my throat

as I brave the cold

toward spring

blood for ink

pools of clear water

soft ripples reflecting light

a little heartbreak

three days cloudy sky

cold seeps slush-like

into bones

sad puddle in my palm

reflects only me

flooded parking lot

early morning rubber boots

splash the world awake

I fell in love precisely

because you asked me not to,

said I was foolish,

one of thousands,

a fly in your soup.

Common.

But you had to concede

that you revealed

yourself to me,

so what I could not control

I revelled in, thinking

one day I'll tell you

what all we have in

Common.

scar tissue raised

beneath cover-up ink

never quite free

finding I had only imagined beauty

taking a sip

of eternal happiness

from an empty cup

the sun shines more brightly

birds sing a sweeter tune

out of spite

My Body

is fertile fleshy flowers

laboured 64 hours

to plant my own tree

a symphony of

pink on pink

blood for ink

cut for love

five full grown fetuses delivered

five personalized livers

five scabs on black sutures

placenta stored in freezers

flayed and remade

of my being

sprouted seedling

clot cascade

pink of pink my body

new life

to make as I like.

chill on the lake

the lone loon

summons the fog

kissed by morning sun,

the sky blushes

feigning innocence

at your touch

heart sutures come undone

too soon

sunset-pink glow

on damp faces

the mourners appear pleased

allow me to tend

the garden of your flesh

where I plant my desire

and grow satisfied

finally free of the look,

I search for

a wandering eye

please, take me instead—

to exchange self for other

is enlightenment

it's so bright because

we are inside the light now

finding our new eyes

you read my story

each and every written word

ignored my warning

dug deeper

past what tempted your desire

down to unyielding

persistent, you stayed

sharpened your tools and waited

for the stone to bleed

seeking less and less, then,

the shore

beyond seeking

tree with exposed roots

barely touching the earth

suddenly, groundlessness

love breaks hearts and bones

for both I use my teeth

you ~~can~~ always count on me to want you

you outgrew your skin

seam split along the spine

unleashed and renewed

blood on earth as in heaven

spilling life like a river

drinking alone

tears don't quench thirst

drifted this far

without considering

the wind

a wound for a heart

overlong unprotected

sleeve rolled up too late

timid sliver

waning

in the blush of dusk

barely breaching the sky

the goddess of light

touches the water

what comes of the rain

unassuming and tender

all

eternity

"the future" is a rope tied off to nothing

the tether

juice dripping

tickle of fuzz

dust on the mason jar

summer rain

lovers search

for a place to hide

oppressive heat—

the light-deprived houseplant

has cool leaves

troublesome youth

kisses all girls

marries none

cardiamnesiac—

feral and

striving against

the tether

through the open window

the whir of air conditioners

tinder typecast

ever reprising

the please love me girl again

fatal crash,

three kilometres away

the storm

headphones in,

I watch the rain

heat wave—

under the covers

with cold toes

drunk love measures

whiskey in lips

not fingers

launderette downtown

big glass windows, change machine

front for laundering

yellow grass—

two minutes of rain

barely wets the pavement

startled by the drop before the storm

a declaration of love

edge of the rooftop

high above the avenue

now who's the coward?

waning august moon

I struggle to describe my suffering

unbounded

listening to the breeze

in the wind sock

unsheathe your navel

and your knife,

the hot and cool

of your affliction

she speaks of

the stray bullet

that nearly took her life

and I hear

a ten year old

who relates her trauma

like a story teller

from a distance

same as me

fresh grass

tearing up fistfuls

we contemplate life

your tense shoulders—

the potential

of our forbidden energy

you vibrate me

at a frequency only you can hear

and you'll wait for me

because that sounds

like love to you

but it's fear

two lips far more sweet

than those already tasted

or, so I assume

my truth is treason–

driven to spill my secrets,

say you'll think poorly of me

jagged scars bind inside to outside

traced by mouth, by absent mind

tangled paths of our own hands

the hands of our enemies

wanderers charting

broken bodies

what I've chained

you unleash

cruel, heartless beast

disguised as the face of love

an uncanny thing

let love wait for me

when I am once again young

my heart will feel free

wheat stalks crumbling

between curious fingers

eager for the fall

merciless harvest

cool autumn tames me

a keen thrill

at the change in the wind

dawn's fog condensed on skin

memories of your desire

searching for comfort—

okay, September

am I hot or cold?

golden leaves wet with rain,

Gran's wheelchair

becomes a sled

golden leaves gather

in thick layers

as I recall

disposing of memories—

into the bin with the rest of you

moldy bale of hay

dust lying thick on leather

the barn years later

tick, tock, telomeres

one anxious beat steals two

the pillow on the pavement

no different from my own

down

fall

merciless harvest

tearful children call down the moon

last of the monarchs

your bitterness lingers

on my tongue

fall leaves carried off by the river

not marrying lust and love

discarded leaves swallow sleet

Mom asks my name

hesitating between two paths—

autumn wind blows the door

open an inch

utterly unknown

I cry without expression

why frown for no one?

my cold tears soundless

in a deserted forest

I haven't slept much

since the day I first saw you.

Please stop haunting me.

smug autumn air

raking leaves over your grave

clear water over old rocks

thinking of you makes me pathetic

seagulls from where?

circling a liminal space

fall leaves line the boulevard—

you were also

a very beautiful

pile of trash

Victoria Encampment:

the pot was destroyed, yet

the plant holds its soil

the wound bloats and weeps

a gangrenous heart, decays

in desolation

our last chance meeting

lonely wind in lonely trees

falling out of love

My Body

craves deep blood secrets

tendons and ligaments

a dull blade

skin to taste

and dirt to swallow

threads to bind me

to the earth

wax, needles

eggs to bury

cold ammonia

a reason to breathe

tragedy, tragedy

tears to wash soiled flesh

blood magic my body

my life

to take as I like.

in ador—

timid

—ation

self-protecting fears

so easily I forget

and call myself brave

brutal wanderer

shut fast the cage

bind yourself within

vigilant nothing gets out

and nothing, *nothing*, gets in

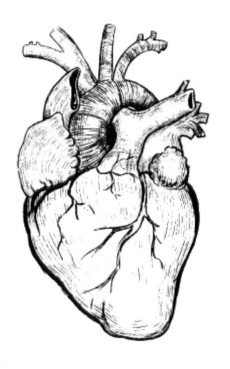

eulogy

1

A fallen log

and a small piece of tin can

with blood on the cutting edge.

A treehouse only big enough for one,

where two make love.

A fire, started with overconfident expertise,

burning brightly while children

smoke and drink like expats.

A secret handshake.

2

A hot-boxed sunroom

in a vacationing neighbour's house.

A flock of grade nines and tens

sprawled drunk and stoned on the carpet.

The 1998 Rob Zombie single "Dragula."

A police officer who responds to the scene.

3

A small purple purse

full of quarter horses

that pay for a cab to the city.

A moon as big and bright

as foreground skyscrapers.

A rooftop campsite, with traps

made of string and shingles.

A pocket knife.

A sweater: a tandem sleeping bag.

A tattoo that says, "always ... forever,"

which stings and has not healed.

4

A wallet on a chain,

dangling from oversized jeans.

A Canadian Forces Parktown bush hat.

A cigarette tucked behind an ear—

an ear where a perfect curl

of sandy blonde hair cups the lobe.

A long, jagged scar winding

from palm to elbow crease.

5

A brick, a nail, a promise.

A fracture.

A tattoo made-over.

A phone call years later.

A bond, a string, a tether, a tear.

An unbroken line.

A knife to the heart.

A "seat at the right hand of God."

6

A suicide.

7

A eulogy.

The poem "hair dryer" (pg 13) first appeared in Scarlet Dragonfly Journal on August 1, 2022.

The poem "pools of clear water" (pg 28) first appeared in Scarlet Dragonfly Journal on October 5, 2022.

scarletdragonflyjournal.wordpress.com

The poem "in ador—" (pg 82) first appeared in Cold Moon Journal on October 19, 2022.

coldmoonjournal.blogspot.com

about the author

anne morrigan is a mother, photographer, minimalist, anime lover, and popcorn addict living in Ontario, Canada.

anne shares poetry, fiction, and articles on haikufeels.com, and #haikufeels poetry prompts daily on twitter.

Made in United States
North Haven, CT
19 July 2025

70841196R00065